THE WORLD
IN THE TIME OF
LEONARDO DA VINCI

Belitha Press

FIONA MACDONALD

First published in the UK in 1997 by

Belitha Press Limited,
London House, Great Eastern Wharf,
Parkgate Road, London SW11 4NQ

ISBN 1 85561 701 3

British Library Cataloguing in Publication Data
for this book is available from the British Library.

Editor: Claire Edwards
Art Director: Helen James
Series Design: Roger Miller
Designer: Ros Saunders
Picture researcher: Diana Morris
Consultant: Sallie Purkis

Printed in Hong Kong
9 8 7 6 5 4 3 2 1

Picture acknowledgements: AKG, London: 4 Biblioteca Reale, Turin.
Bridgeman Art Library: front cover l British Library, London;
back cover British Museum, London; 1cl St Peter's Vatican Collection;
1cr Giraudon/Biblioteca Nacional, Madrid; 2 American Museum of Natural
History, New York; 5t Museo di Firenze Com'era; 6b Bibliothèque de
l'Institut de France, Paris; 12 Bibliothèque Nationale, Paris;
14b British Museum, London; 16 British Library, London; 17b
Biblioteca Nacional, Madrid; 19b Palazzo Medici-Riccardi, Florence;
22t Victoria & Albert Museum, London; 22b Royal Geographical
Society, London; 23r Giraudon/Biblioteca Nacional, Madrid; 25t
British Library, London; 28 National Library of Australia, Canberra;
29t British Museum, London; 29b American Museum of Natural History,
New York; 30 Stapleton College; 31t Raymond O'Shea Gallery, London;
31b British Library, London; 32b Chester Beatty Library, Dublin; 34 Victoria &
Albert Museum, London; 36 St Peter's Vatican Collection; 37t National Gallery,
London; 37b **Bridgeman Art Library**: Uffizi Gallery, Florence; 38l British
Library, London; 39t, 40b, 41t, 41c, 45l British Museum, London. **British
Museum, London**: 5b. **E.T. Archive**: 3 Louvre, Paris; 6t Czartorysky Museum,
Cracow; 7b Louvre, Paris; 13 Moldovita Monstery, Romania; 17t University
Museum, Cuzco; 18 El Prado, Madrid; 19t British Museum, London;

Picture acknowledgments cont: 23l Pedro de Osma Museum, Lima; 24
Torre Aquila, Trento; 25b University Library, Istanbul; 35t; 42 National Museum,
Copenhagen. **Werner Forman Archive**: 1c British Museum, London;
15 Kuroda Collection, Japan; 20r British Museum, London; 26t; 33 Kozu
Collection, Kyoto; 39b Private Collection; 45r Biblioteca Universitaria,
Bologna. **Sonia Halliday Photographs**: 20l Topkapi Palace Museum, Istanbul;
26b James Wellard; 38r. **Robert Harding Picture Library**: 21t Schuster;
44 Michael Jenner. **Copyright reserved to HM The Queen**: 7t. **Michael
Holford**: 43. **Images of India**: 40t N.M. Kelva. **Japan Archive**: 21b. **N.J.
Saunders**: 35b. **Scala**: front cover r. **Topkapi Palace Museum, Istanbul**:
32t. **University of Tokyo**: 27.

CONTENTS

The Story of Leonardo da Vinci 4

The World 1450–1550 8

Time Line 10

Around the World 12

Famous Rulers and Leaders 18

How People Lived 24

Discovery and Invention 30

The Creative World 36

Beliefs and Ideas 42

Glossary 46

Index 48

ABOUT THIS BOOK

This book tells the story of Leonardo da Vinci, and also looks at what was happening all around the world in his time. To help you find your way through the book, each chapter has been divided into seven sections. Each section describes a different part of the world, and is headed by a colour bar. As you look through a chapter, the colour bars tell you which area you can read about in the text below. There is a time line, to give you an outline of world events in Leonardo's time, and also a map, which shows some of the most important places mentioned in the book.

On page 46 there is a list of some of the peoples you will come across in this book. Some of the more unfamiliar words are also listed in the glossary.

THE STORY OF LEONARDO

▲ Leonardo painted this picture of a serious and thoughtful old man when he himself was getting old. Like the picture of Leonardo on the cover, people think that this is a self-portrait, but no one knows for sure.

Leonardo da Vinci was born more than 500 years ago, but his name is still remembered today, and his achievements are admired all round the world. No one else in Leonardo's time studied so many different topics, and had so many brilliant ideas. This book tells you a little about his life as an artist, a scientist and an engineer. It also tells you what was happening elsewhere in the world in Leonardo's time.

Leonardo lived from 1452 to 1519, but this book covers a longer time span, from about 1450 to 1550. It will help you to find out about events that shaped the world before Leonardo was born, and to discover what happened in the years after he died.

A DIFFICULT START

Leonardo did not have a good start in life. His mother was a peasant woman called Caterina, and his father, Piero da Vinci, was a lawyer. They were not married, but Piero da Vinci took young Leonardo into his family, and brought him up.

A NEW HOME IN FLORENCE

Around 1469 Leonardo moved with his father and stepmother to Florence, one of the richest and most splendid cities in Italy. Florence was a centre of trade and industry, especially for fine woollen cloth. Some of Italy's richest merchants lived there, in huge palaces. They paid for new houses, churches, fountains and gardens, and filled them with wonderful pictures and statues.

▲ The city of Florence in the 1500s. It was a great business centre, and many of Europe's earliest banks were set up there. Florence was governed by a rich family called the Medici. They encouraged the best artists to come and work in the city.

AN APPRENTICESHIP

Even as a child Leonardo liked drawing and was very good at it. So his father arranged for him to become an apprentice in the studio of a famous painter in Florence called Andrea Verrocchio. An apprenticeship was the usual way for boys, and some girls, to train for a skilled craft. They went to live with a master artist or craftworker and helped with the work. In return the master fed and clothed them and taught them all his skills.

SCIENCE AND ART

For the next ten years, Leonardo worked hard. Sometimes he helped Verrocchio in his studio, sometimes he worked by himself. He studied science and engineering, and learned how to build bridges, dig canals and design weapons. He painted, carved sculptures, and was a fine musician.

◄ Leonardo was trained in a studio like this one. At the front of the picture you can see an artist entertaining a rich customer. All around you can see his assistants and apprentices designing frescoes, carving statues and grinding coloured earth to make paints.

FESTIVALS AND MAGIC MACHINES

In 1492 Leonardo moved to Milan. He went to work for the ruler, the Duke of Milan, helping to arrange festivals at the palace – with magic machines, special effects and music. When he wasn't working for the duke, he continued with his studies. Leonardo made hundreds of sketches in his notebooks, of plants, animals and the human body. He was fascinated to see how things fitted together and how they worked.

◀ While Leonardo was in Milan, he painted many pictures. This one is a portrait of the duke's girlfriend, a fashionable Italian woman called Cecilia Galleriani. She is holding her pet stoat.

A NEW STYLE FULL OF SHADOWS

Leonardo used the information from his studies in his pictures. Stories were told about how he made collections of dead snakes, lizards and toads so that he could paint them in a lifelike way. He concentrated so hard on his studies that he did not notice when the dead bodies began to rot and smell. Leonardo also began to develop his own way of painting at this time. People called it *sfumato*, which means 'smoky.' All Leonardo's people were painted in a misty, mysterious way, and his paintings were full of dark shadows.

▼ One of Leonardo's many designs for new inventions. This is a flying machine. Leonardo has made detailed sketches, showing how the machine will work.

FAME IN FLORENCE

In 1500 Leonardo moved back to Florence, where he worked for the Medici family as a map-maker and engineer, and continued to paint in his own special style. By now he was very famous. At about this time, Leonardo painted his most famous portrait, called the *Mona Lisa*. It is still one of the best-known pictures in the world, although people disagree about its effect. Some call it magical and beautiful, but others find the fantasy landscape and Mona Lisa's half-closed eyes and secretive smile strange and disturbing.

ART AND SCIENCE

In Florence Leonardo also continued his studies. He believed that art and science should not be kept separate, but that each topic he studied would help him with all his other work. He kept a collection of notebooks (more than 3,500 pages in total) full of scientific observations and experiments. He also made sketches of his engineering designs. He wrote in backwards mirror-writing, possibly to keep his notes secret, but also because he was left-handed and it was quicker and easier for him to write that way.

▲ A page from one of Leonardo's notebooks showing drawings of a hand, arm and shoulder. Like other artists, he often cut up, then sketched, dead bodies.

WORKING FOR THE KING OF FRANCE

Between 1506 and 1513 Leonardo worked in Florence and in Milan. In 1516 he was invited by King Francis I of France to advise him on some new building plans. Francis was interested in art and admired Leonardo's work. Leonardo accepted eagerly, and soon thought up all kinds of exciting new projects for the French king. These included a massive plan to control the flow of the River Loire. But he died, after less than three years in France, before he could complete the plans. All over Europe people mourned him. They realized that Leonardo had been one of the most creative and inventive minds of his time.

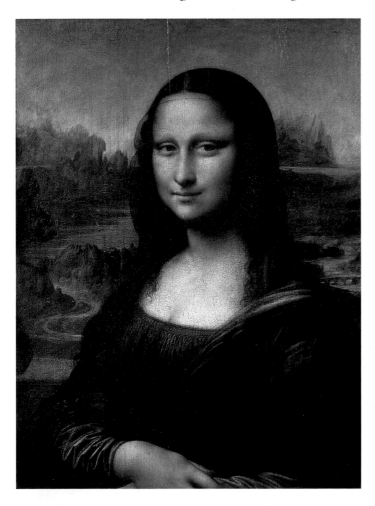

▲ Leonardo's most famous portrait, the *Mona Lisa*, which he painted between 1503 and 1506. Leonardo was always trying out new techniques. Here he has used such fine brushwork that you cannot see the separate strokes.

THE WORLD 1450-1550

ABOUT THE MAPS

The maps on this page will help you find your way around the world in Lonardo da Vinci's time. The big map shows some of the places mentioned in the text, including:

• **COUNTRIES** that are different from modern ones, such as Persia and Benin.

• *Past peoples*, such as the Incas and Aztecs.

• *GEOGRAPHICAL FEATURES*, including mountains and rivers.

• *Towns and cities.* To find the position of a town or city, look for the name in the list below then find the number on the map.

1 Tenochtitlán	9 Florence	15 Kilwa
2 Machu Picchu	10 Constantinople (Istanbul)	16 Samarkand
3 Cuzco		17 Kabul
4 Bruges	11 Timbuktu	18 Delhi
5 Antwerp	12 Mecca	19 Malacca
6 Mainz	13 Mombasa	20 Beijing
7 Venice	14 Great Zimbabwe	21 Hangzhou
8 Milan		22 Kyoto

The little map shows the world divided into seven regions. The people who lived there were linked by customs, traditions, beliefs, or simply by their environment. There were many differences within each region, but the people living there had more in common with each other than with people elsewhere. Each region is shown in a different colour – the same colours are used in the headings throughout the book.

ARCTIC
OCEAN

Mongols

EUROPE

4 5 6

8 7
9

10 BLACK SEA

OTTOMAN EMPIRE

A   S   I   A

GOBI
DESERT

16

20

22

HIMALAYAS

17

21

PERSIA

MING
CHINA

MEDITERRANEAN
SEA

Bedouin

NILE

12

INDUS GANGES

18

11 SAHARA
DESERT

SONGHAY

AFRICA

ARABIAN
SEA   *Vijayanagar*

SOUTH CHINA SEA

PACIFIC
OCEAN

MALI

BENIN

13

19

EQUATOR

INDIAN

OCEAN

Pacific peoples

15

AUSTRALASIA

14

San

Aboriginals

Maoris

KEY TO MAP

	Africa
	Americas
	Australasia
	East Asia
	Europe
	Middle East
	South Asia

TIME LINE

1450   1475

EUROPE

1455–1485 The Wars of the Roses in England.

1490 Ballet-dancing invented in Italy.

1444–1510 Sandro Botticelli, a famous Italian Renaissance artist.

c.1460 New sailing ships, called carracks are designed for long sea voyages.

1462–1505 Reign of Ivan the Great of Moscow, who founds the Russian state.

1452 Leonardo da Vinci born.

1453 End of Hundred Years War between England and France.

1475–1564 Michaelangelo Buonarotti, an Italian Renaissance sculptor, painter, architect and poet.

1455 Johann Gutenburg produces the first printed Bible in Germany.

1483–1564 Martin Luther, German leader of Church reform.

MIDDLE EAST

1453 Ottoman Turks capture Constantinople and rename it Istanbul.

1450 Mocha, in Arabia, becomes the world's main coffee trading port.

1451–1481 Mehmet the Conqueror rules the Ottoman Empire.

AFRICA

1464–1591 Songhay Empire rules a large area of West Africa. One of its biggest cities, Timbuktu, becomes a great centre of trade, education and Islamic culture.

1481–1504 Oba Ozuolua expands the Benin Empire.

c.1450 The palace-city of Great Zimbabwe, East Africa, begins to be abandoned.

1465 Songhay conquers Mali.

1486 Portuguese explorers arrive in the city of Benin.

EAST ASIA

c.1467–1477 Onin War between rival Japanese warlords. Civil wars in Japan continue for next 100 years.

1490 Takamoto-Bokuden, one of the most famous swordsmen ever, born in Japan.

1418–1450 King Sejong rules Korea. Invents a new Korean alphabet, called hangul. It is still used today.

1473 Shogun Yoshimasa of Japan gives up power. Spends the rest of his life encouraging the arts.

SOUTH ASIA

1469–1539 Guru Nanak, founder of the Sikh faith.

c.1450 Hindu kingdom of Vijayanagar powerful in southern India.

1471 Vietnamese Empire expands southwards.

AUSTRALASIA

1500 Chinese sailors may have reached the north coast of Australia by this time and traded with the Aboriginal peoples who lived there.

1450–1550 Migration continues between various islands in the Pacific Ocean.

c.1450 Maoris continue to migrate from North Island to South Island of New Zealand.

AMERICAS

1440–1468 Montezuma I expands Aztec Empire.

1470 Incas conquer Chimu nation (in present-day northern Peru).

1438–1471 Emperor Pachacuti expands Inca Empire.

c.1450 Incas build fortress city of Machu Picchu in Andes Mountains.

1492 Columbus sails to America. He thinks he has reached East Asia.

1500   **1525**   **1550**

1494 Spain and Portugal agree to divide between them all new lands that European explorers reach in America and the Far East.

1497–1543 Hans Holbein the Younger, an important Renaissance artist from northern Europe.

1509–1564 John Calvin, French leader of Church reform.

1512–1594 Map-maker known as Mercator, the first person to make maps that show the whole world on a flat sheet of paper.

1519 Ferdinand Magellan sets off from Spain to sail round the world.

1519 Leonardo da Vinci dies.

1509–1547 King Henry VIII rules England amd Wales.

1520 First state lottery begins in France.

1543 Copernicus publishes a book claiming that the earth travels round the sun. (Later banned by the Church.)

1499 War between Ottoman Turks and Venice, Italy.

1501 Ismail I conquers Persia and declares himself shah (king). His dynasty, the Safavids, rule until 1722.

1509 Istanbul destroyed by earthquake.

1514 War between Turks and Persians.

1516–1517 Ottoman Turks conquer Syria and Arabia.

1520–1566 Suleiman the Magnificent rules the Ottoman Empire.

1526 Turks conquer Hungary.

1505 Portuguese capture the rich trading city of Kilwa on East African coast.

1509 Portuguese build forts on the West African coast.

1510 First African slaves are transported to the Caribbean.

1517 Ottoman Turks conquer Egypt.

1510–1540 Hausa kingdoms become powerful in West Africa.

1535 Charles V, Holy Roman Emperor, conquers Tunis on North African coast.

1522–1591 Sen-No-Rikyu, the most famous master of the Japanese tea ceremony. He believed that the calm mood the ceremony created was more important than the implements used.

1543 First record of Europeans landing in Japan, blown there by a storm.

1550 Japanese and Chinese pirate raids on Chinese coast.

1550 Mongols invade northern China.

1498 Portuguese explorer Vasco da Gama sails round the southern tip of Africa and across the Indian Ocean to reach India.

c.1500 Muslim sultans rule Sumatra and Java.

1511 Portuguese explorers arrive in Thailand.

1511 Portuguese traders settle in Malacca (in present-day Malaysia).

1521 Magellan is killed fighting in local war in Philippines.

1526 Babur conquers North India and founds Mughal Empire.

1520 Portuguese explorer Ferdinand Magellan becomes the first European to sail round South America and enter the Pacific Ocean.

1526 Portuguese sailors arrive in Papua New Guinea.

1497 English explorer John Cabot lands in Newfoundland, Canada, and claims the territory for England.

1507 The word America is used on a map for the first time, after Italian explorer Amerigo Vespucci, who proved America was a new continent in the west and not part of Asia.

1519 First chocolate sent to Spain from Mexico.

1519–1521 Hernán Cortés conquers Aztec Empire.

1532–1533 Francisco Pizarro conquers Inca Empire.

1550 By now potatoes and tobacco have reached Europe from the Americas.

c.1550 Five Native nations in North-east America form the Iroquois League.

AROUND THE WORLD

For most of Leonardo's lifetime much of the world was at war. Sometimes wars were fought when powerful kingdoms or city-states tried to conquer their weaker neighbours. Sometimes there were fights between rival religious groups, or between princes quarrelling over who should be king.

This was also a time when adventurers and explorers, mostly from Spain and Portugal, were beginning to make contact with parts of the world that Europeans had not known about before. They were seeking treasure and trade, and hoping to find the quickest way to sail from Europe to rich Asian lands on the other side of the world.

▲ This manuscript illustration shows French and English soldiers fighting during the Hundred Years War, which lasted from 1337 to 1453. (The French are on the right.) Knights on horseback are wearing heavy metal armour. They are fighting against ordinary soldiers armed with deadly longbows.

A HUNDRED YEARS OF WAR

For many years England and France had been fighting over England's claim to rule parts of France. In 1453, just after Leonardo was born, peace was finally agreed and England lost its claim. The war, which became known as the Hundred Years War, brought death and disaster to ordinary French people. Their farms were destroyed and their cities were looted by armies, which often ran out of control.

THE WARS OF THE ROSES

Despite the fighting between kingdoms and cities, parts of Europe were growing rich. Many towns such as Bruges, Antwerp and Venice, were all great centres of trade. In England there was a successful cloth-making industry. But only two years after France and England had made peace, many parts of the country were caught up in a civil war. Rival nobles struggled over who should rule England, and there were outbreaks of fighting between 1455 and 1485. The fighting became known as the Wars of the Roses, after the red and white rose badges that some of the rival soldiers wore.

THE FALL OF CONSTANTINOPLE

The Ottoman dynasty was founded around 1300 by a Turkish war-leader called Osman I. At first the Ottoman sultans ruled only a small kingdom in Turkey, but by Leonardo's time their Muslim empire had become the most powerful state in eastern Europe, North Africa and the Middle East. In 1453 the Ottomans captured Constantinople, a city that had been ruled by Christian emperors for a thousand years. They renamed it Istanbul and made it their capital city. The sultans lived there in splendid palaces, hung with beautiful Middle Eastern silks and carpets.

▼ This wall-painting shows Ottoman Turkish troops surrounding the walled city of Constantinople. The last Christian emperor died fighting with his soldiers at the top of the city walls.

RUNNING THE EMPIRE

MIDDLE EAST

The Ottoman Empire was run by well-trained slaves. Some were bought from slave traders, others were captured in war. But the top jobs in the army and the civil service were filled by slaves specially recruited from Christian lands. Officers chose the strongest, most intelligent and best-looking boys. Some trained as fierce, brilliant soldiers, called janissaries. Others were taught Turkish, Persian and Arabic (the languages spoken in the empire), law, history and philosophy. When they had qualified, they worked as local governors, tax collectors and administrators. The cleverest were sent to Istanbul to become political advisers to the sultan and his court.

▲ The city of Timbuktu grew rich as a centre of trade. Merchants travelling by camel across the Sahara Desert stayed in fine houses there. The houses were designed in both African and Arabic styles.

THE OBAS OF BENIN

AFRICA

The kingdom of Benin in western Africa first became powerful around 1400. During Leonardo's lifetime, the obas (kings) of Benin led their armies to conquer new villages and land. They surrounded their capital city, also called Benin, with massive earthworks, and huge walls to defend it. The city of Benin was a great centre of trade. The obas built new markets, and encouraged well-organized groups of craftworkers to live and work for them there. Metalwork and cloth from Benin were highly prized, and Benin traders were famous for their business skills. For money, they used beautiful cowrie shells fished from the sea.

EXPLORERS FROM PORTUGAL

During the 1400s explorers from Portugal sailed down the west coast of Africa, and reached the city of Benin in 1486. They hoped to find gold, but gold was mined in other African kingdoms, such as Mali and Songhay. So the Portuguese bought slaves from Benin traders instead.

Thousands of miles away, on the East African coast, merchants from Arabia, India and even China traded with the rich cities of Kilwa and Mombasa. They also made contact with gold miners, cattle-keepers and craftworkers who lived in the rich inland kingdom of Zimbabwe.

◄ This brass plaque from Benin, probably made in the 1500s, shows an oba. He is holding two fierce leopards as a sign of his royal power.

MING RULERS

China was ruled by the Ming dynasty. In 1368 the first Ming emperor had ended over 100 years of foreign rule by driving Mongol armies from his land. From then on the Ming emperors had three main aims – to rebuild their kingdom's strength and wealth, to encourage Chinese customs and civilization, and to keep all foreign armies and any foreign influence out of their lands.

▼ A typical scene in war-torn Japan. Samurai warriors on horseback lead their armies to surround a rival warlord's castle. This picture was painted later, when much of the fighting was over.

CIVIL WAR

In Japan, as in Europe, there were bitter civil wars that lasted from about 1350 to 1600, as rival warlords, called samurai, struggled for power. Samurai were well-trained and followed a warrior code in which bravery and honour were more important than anything else. They kept their own private armies and lived in fine castles. Samurai who lived on the sea coast led cruel and fearless pirate fleets. Because there was no strong government, the country was full of bandit gangs.

In 1543 the first-known Europeans landed in Japan. They were soon followed by traders and by Christian missionaries, but after less than 100 years, the Japanese drove all foreigners away.

INVASION

During the 1400s India and the nearby lands were divided into several kingdoms, including Delhi in the north, ruled by Muslims, and the Hindu empire of Vijayanagar in the south. There were also many powerful independent princes. In 1526 Babur, a warrior prince from Central Asia, invaded India and conquered the rich city of Delhi and all its lands.

NEW TRADE

In South-east Asia, merchants traded with travellers from many lands. The first European merchant ships began to arrive in South Asian ports and the Europeans set up trading posts there. They carried valuable goods from the east, such as spices, cloth and jewels, more quickly and easily than earlier merchants travelling overland.

HUNTING AND TRADING

The Aboriginal peoples of Australia were skilful hunters, fishermen and trappers. They lived in close-knit family groups. At times when there was plenty of food, families met together to exchange news, sort out disputes, and trade food and goods they had made. People living on the north coast of Australia traded with sailors from Indonesia and from islands in the Indian Ocean. The Indonesians were in contact with Arabian spice traders and, after 1520, with explorers from Europe, too.

▼ The Portuguese trading post at Malacca, in the Spice Islands. You can see the governor's big house and a Christian church inside the strong walls. Outside the walls there are merchant houses, storerooms, and rainforest trees.

MALACA.

CITIES IN THE NORTH

AMERICAS

North America was home to about 300 Native American peoples in Leonardo's time. They all led different lifestyles, from the trading cities along the Mississippi River valley, to the Inuit villages in the icy north.

Although Viking traders had reached North America hundreds of years before, people in Leonardo's time did not know this. For them, the first contact between Europe and the Americas was Columbus' journey there in 1492.

THE AZTECS

A warlike people called the Aztecs lived in present-day Mexico and ruled a mighty empire. Conquered peoples paid Aztec rulers tribute – gold dust, cocoa beans, jaguar skins and precious feathers from tropical birds. The Aztecs called themselves the Mexica. They were skilful builders, farmers and craftworkers. For safety, they built their capital city, Tenochtitlán, in the middle of a lake. Almost a quarter of a million people lived there in Leonardo da Vinci's time.

► This silver figure was made by a craftworker living in the Inca capital city of Cuzco. It was made for a rich person to give as an offering to the gods.

THE INCAS

The Incas ruled over an empire that stretched 3,500 kilometres along the Pacific coast. The capital city was Cuzco, in present-day Peru. From there, Inca emperors ruled over a well-organized workforce. Peasants farmed the rugged mountainsides. Craftworkers made magnificent buildings and works of art in precious metals.

The last Inca ruler, Atahualpa, had to defend his lands against Spanish treasure-seekers. They were armed with guns that were far more powerful than the Incas' clubs. Thousands of Incas also died of diseases brought by the Europeans. Atahualpa was captured by Spanish soldiers in 1532. Even though his loyal subjects collected an enormous fortune in gold and silver to offer as a ransom, the Spaniards executed him in 1533 and took control of the empire.

◄ In this painting Aztec warriors are being led by an important noble called an eagle knight. He is wearing a special uniform made out of an eagle's feathered skin. The Aztec armies terrified many Central American peoples, but in 1521 they were defeated by Spanish soldiers led by Hernán Cortés.

FAMOUS RULERS AND LEADERS

The rulers and leaders who lived in Leonardo's time were keen to conquer more land and build up huge empires. But many warlike rulers, such as the Ottoman Sultan Suleiman and the Mughal Emperor Babur, were also great patrons of art and literature. They spent vast amounts of money encouraging artists and craftworkers to produce great works. Jewels, portaits and palaces created a good image, and showed how rich and strong the rulers were.

Many rulers were also genuinely interested in art, and liked the company of great artists. The Holy Roman Emperor Charles V even made the brilliant Italian painter Titian a nobleman in 1533, because he liked his work so much.

▲ This picture of Charles V was painted by the Italian painter Titian. It shows Charles as a powerful leader. He ruled as Holy Roman Emperor from 1519 to 1556, and collected more land, through diplomacy and war, than any other European ruler before.

LORENZO DE MEDICI

EUROPE

In Leonardo's time Italy was made up of many city-states. One of the most important was Florence. It was a republic, ruled by the powerful Medici family, who made money from banking. Lorenzo de Medici ruled Florence from 1469 to 1492. He was famous throughout Europe for his love of the arts. He invited artists, architects, scholars, writers, musicans and philosophers to eat with him every day, so that he could keep up to date with the latest ideas. He also gave public entertainments for the people of Florence to enjoy. Lorenzo believed that beautiful surroundings would help people live better lives. He worked with other rich citizens to rule the city wisely and well.

▶ Lorenzo de Medici was one of the greatest patrons of art in Leonardo's time. This terracotta statue of him was made by Verrocchio, who taught Leonardo to paint.

▲ King Henry VIII liked music and wrote several tunes, including 'Greensleeves'. Here he is shown with his court jester, Will Summers. Henry is playing the harp.

KING HENRY VIII

King Henry VIII ruled England and Wales from 1509 to 1547. He was praised as a typical Renaissance prince. He was well-educated, spoke several languages, was fond of music and art, and was brave on the battlefield. He was also keen on hunting and on tennis – a new sport at the time.

A NEW WIFE AND NEW RELIGION

Henry VIII was interested in religious arguments in Europe (see page 43), and at first supported the Roman Catholic Church. But when the pope refused to allow him to divorce his wife and marry again, he decided to separate the English Church from the rule of the pope in Rome. He married Anne Boleyn, and set up a new Church of England with himself as its head. Anne Boleyn had a daughter, but no sons, so Henry had her executed and married again. His third wife had a son, who became King Edward VI, but in 1558 Henry and Anne's daughter became a much greater ruler – Elizabeth I of England.

THE CONQUEROR

Ottoman Sultan
Mehmet II, nicknamed The Conqueror, ruled
from 1451 to 1481. He became sultan when he
was only 19, and led the armies that captured the
city of Constantinople. He spent most of his life
fighting. By the end of his reign, the Ottoman
Empire was larger and stronger than ever before.

THE MAGNIFICENT LAWMAKER

Sultan Suleiman I was born in 1494. He ruled
from 1520 to 1566, and was another great
Ottoman war-leader. His warships controlled
the Mediterranean Sea. In Europe he became
known as Suleiman the Magnificent, because he
spent so much money as a patron of architecture
and the arts. In the Ottoman lands he earned the
name Suleiman the Lawmaker, because he
reformed the Ottoman system of government,
and passed many new laws.

OZUOLUA'S DOWNFALL

Oba Ozuolua, who ruled Benin from 1481
to 1504, expanded his empire by conquering
nearby lands belonging to rival peoples. But after
many years of war his soldiers began to feel that
Ozuola cared only for his own glory, and did not
mind how many people died. So they shot him
with a poisoned arrow. They did this while
Ozuola was having a bath, because it was one
of the few times he took his armour off.

FIGHTING FOR POWER

The obas of Benin had many wives.
When an oba died there was often
a struggle between the sons of
different mothers over who
should be the next ruler. After
Ozuolua's death his son Esigie
had to fight to become oba.
Esigie preferred to spend his
time peacefully. He
encouraged craftworkers
and helped trade. He
made friends with
Portuguese merchants
and probably spoke
Portuguese.

► Queen Idia of Benin,
Oba Esigie's mother. The
artist has shown her
wearing a royal headdress
made of coral beads. Esigie
gave his mother an important
role in ruling the country, and
built a special palace for her.

◄ Mehmet the Conqueror is shown
here, wearing rich royal robes. Artists often
painted their rulers holding a rose to show
that they were not just warriors, but men
of taste who enjoyed beauty too.

MONGOLS AND THE MING

EAST ASIA

In the years before Leonardo was born, China was ruled by a wise and powerful emperor called Ming Yongle. But he died in 1424, and the emperors of the Ming dynasty who ruled after him were much less successful. One, called Cheng Tung, set off north in 1449 to fight the Mongols. They captured him and the government had to pay a lot of money before he was set free. After this the Mongols were angry at being attacked, and invaded China. At the same time, pirate leaders who sailed in the South China Sea took advantage of these fights to attack Chinese merchant ships. For many years after Cheng Tung's adventure, Chinese rulers had to spend most of their time trying to defend their lands.

CIVIL WAR

In Japan, although there was an emperor, the country was really ruled by a warrior leader, called a shogun. One family, the Ashikaga, had ruled for more than 100 years, but in 1466 they fought among themselves over who should be the next shogun. This led to a war that almost destroyed the emperor's royal city of Kyoto. In 1470 the ruling shogun, called Yoshimasa, retired to his palace on the outskirts of Kyoto and spent his time with Japan's best artists, poets and musicians. Other warlord families battled on for the title of shogun. The fighting was finally ended by General Oda Nobunaga.

▲ Chinese rulers lived in this palace in Beijing. In the 1400s the old mud and straw walls were replaced with solid stone, and many beautiful halls and temples were built. The palace was called the Forbidden City, because ordinary people were not allowed in.

▼ General Oda Nobunaga, who lived from 1534 to 1582, helped to end the long years of civil war in Japan. He forced most of the warrior leaders to obey his commands. He is shown here looking very fierce in full armour.

BABUR'S CONQUESTS

Babur was born in Central Asia, in 1483, and founded a mighty empire in India. When he was only 14 years old he led a successful raid on the rich city of Samarkand, and in 1504, when he was 21, he captured the important fortress of Kabul, in present-day Afghanistan. By 1526 he had conquered the Sultanate of Delhi. He died fighting in 1530, by which time he controlled most of northern India.

Babur was brave and ruthless – his name means Tiger. But he could also be thoughtful and sensitive. He loved books, pictures, poetry and jewels. He was descended from two great Mongol warlords called Timur and Chingiz Khan. The dynasty he founded became known as Mughal, which meant Mongol in Persian, the language spoken by many scholars in India.

▲ This painting, made in 1528, shows the first Mughal emperor Babur in a garden with his courtiers. Babur collected many rare and beautiful plants.

ELDERS AND WAR LEADERS

We do not know the names of any leaders among the Aboriginal people of Australia or of the Maoris in New Zealand. But traditions and stories tell us a little about what their duties may have been. Family groups were guided by elders. These were older people who passed on their experience, and kept younger people under control. Maori chiefs were war-leaders. They had to be ready to avenge an insult, to defend their homes and families, or to win honour by killing their enemies on surprise raids.

◄ Maori chiefs had to defend their villages and farms from enemy warrior bands. This picture was painted after Leonardo's time, but shows clothes and weapons that had changed little since then.

BUILDING THE INCA EMPIRE

The Inca ruler Pachacuti Yupanqui behaved like many other leaders in Leonardo's time. He planned and led a series of wars to make his empire bigger, and conquered many nearby lands. But to the Inca people, Pachacuti was more than just a brilliant battle commander. He was the son of the Sun, and had absolute power. To keep their god-like blood pure, Inca kings only married other family members, although many had extra wives as well.

▲ Pachacuti ruled the Inca empire from 1438 to 1471. He was a brilliant leader and organizer. There were no paintings of Inca rulers made at the time, and this later picture was painted by a European in about 1750. It is based on traditional stories about Pachacuti, and on travellers' descriptions of Inca clothes and jewels.

▼ Montezuma II ruled the Aztec Empire from 1502 to 1520. This picture of him is from an Aztec book called a codex. He is shown here being crowned.

MONTEZUMA II

Early Aztec rulers were bold warriors, but Montezuma II, who came to power in 1502, was more interested in religion. When Spanish conquerers landed in Mexico in 1519, he thought they were gods, and refused to fight. So the Spaniards put him in prison. Other Aztec leaders tried to drive the Spaniards out of their lands, but they failed. Montezuma died mysteriously during the fighting, in 1520. No one knows whether he was killed by the Spaniards, or by his own people who were angry because he wouldn't fight.

HOW PEOPLE LIVED

▲ This Italian painting shows peasant men and women busy harvesting wheat. Inside the city wall at the front of the picture, well-dressed nobles look on.

Leonardo lived in Florence, one of the richest cities in Europe. Its rulers and citizens were rich enough to pay for fine buildings and beautiful works of art, and also for schemes to provide food and money for poor people who came to their city in search of help.

All round the world there were great gaps in living standards between the rich and the poor. Some governments, like the Incas in South America, set up state welfare schemes. Some rulers, like the kings of England and France, tried to solve the problem of homeless beggars by passing strict laws. Religious leaders from many faiths taught that charity was a holy duty. But often people who were too ill to work, or who had no money, had to rely on their families and friends, or else starve.

▲ This manuscript illustration shows sheep being sheared. Many farmers in northern Europe grew rich by keeping flocks of sheep and selling their wool.

TOWN LIFE

EUROPE

Life in a European town could be comfortable for rich people, such as nobles, lawyers, top churchmen, successful merchants and craftworkers. They could all afford a large house in a quiet street, good food from the markets, and servants to look after them. Poor people lived in overcrowded homes. The backstreets were often full of dirt and disease.

POVERTY AND PROBLEMS

Most people in Europe lived in the countryside. They worked as farm labourers, or as servants in big houses. Their lives became even harder after around 1500. The population began to grow, so there was less food to go round and it became more expensive. At the same time wages fell, because there were lots of people looking for work and not enough jobs. In England, Belgium and Germany there were riots. The poorest people were often starving. Some people were driven to stealing money, goods, or even food. Governments reacted by passing harsh new laws.

FARMS AND TOWNS

MIDDLE EAST

In the Middle Eastern countryside farmers lived in small villages. They raised sheep and goats, and planted orchards of apricots, almonds and olives. Where soils were rich and there was a good water supply, they grew wheat, barley, grapes, figs and melons. Oxen were used to pull ploughs, and donkeys carried loads up steep mountain tracks.

Craftworkers and merchants lived in busy trading towns, where there were huge covered markets, called souks. Visitors could buy everyday clothes and household items, or the most expensive silks, jewels and perfumes in the world.

▲ A town in Turkey. Towns in the Middle East were well-planned, with schools, hospitals and travellers' lodges. In the picture you can see six mosques, with their domed roofs and minarets. At the front left of the picture is the governor's palace.

DESERT TRADE

In Middle Eastern desert lands people kept camels for transport and to provide meat and milk. Rich, sticky fruit grew on wild date palms at oases, created by natural springs. Frankincense and myrrh trees were also grown for their valuable, sweet-smelling gum. The Arabian people, called Bedouin, followed an ancient nomadic lifestyle. They lived in tents made from woven goats' hair, and earned money by breeding camels, horses and hunting dogs. They also led trains of camels loaded with precious spices, gold, gemstones and pearls across the deserts to trade at busy sea ports.

TOWNS AND VILLAGES

There were many rich and thriving towns in Africa, including Timbuktu and Benin. But most people in Africa made their living from the land. In the tropical rainforests of West and Central Africa, farmers cleared fields to grow vegetables such as yams and plantains. In drier, cooler regions, such as Zimbabwe, people grew crops of millet and sorghum, which they pounded and mixed with boiled water to make a kind of porridge.

Women usually sowed and harvested the crops, cooked, and fetched water from rivers or wells. It was hard and tiring work, especially as they had to look after their children and clean their houses as well. In the driest regions of Africa food crops would not grow, so cattle were the main source of food. Cattle were usually looked after by men.

▲ Many edible plants, such as mangoes and plantains, grew wild in West Africa. This bronze plaque from Benin shows a servant climbing a tree to gather fruit.

NOMAD LIFE

In nomad communities, such as the San in southern Africa, men herded cattle and hunted. They tracked or trapped wild animals and birds, and killed them with spears, or bows and arrows, sometimes tipped with poison. Women gathered fruits, roots and wild honey for food.

► People had herded cattle for thousands of years in many parts of Africa, and little had changed by Leonardo's time. This ancient rock painting shows African herdsmen and their cattle.

RICE TAXES IN JAPAN

EAST ASIA

Rice was the staple food for most people living in East Asia. Rice was so important that in Japan it was used to measure a nobleman's wealth. Peasants often paid their taxes to landowners in rice. This could be up to half the crop, and peasants sometimes rioted in protest.

Growing rice was exhausting and skilful work. Peasants had to stand ankle-deep in water in flooded fields to plant the rice seedlings. They had to control very carefully how much water flowed into the fields to be sure of a successful crop. When the rice was ripe the fields were drained and the long rice stalks cut. They were carted to the farmyard to be dried and threshed.

▼ In the picture, Japanese women are beating bunches of rice against straw matting to separate the grains of rice from the stalks. Behind them, men are polishing the grains by turning them in a big mill.

HOUSEBOATS AND PEARL FISHING

The Chinese population more than doubled in size between 1400 and 1550. This meant more demand for food and clothing. Peasants cleared new land, planned new irrigation schemes, and planted new crops, such as cotton. Around the coast and on China's rivers and canals, many families lived on boats. They made money from fishing, ferrying travellers, or transporting heavy loads. Sometimes children were kidnapped by merchants and forced to work as divers, gathering pearl oysters from the sea bed. Many drowned.

BIG CITIES

In China, there were many large cities and towns, such as Hangzhou and Beijing, where people earned a living from making craft goods, and from trade. In Japan, the city of Kyoto was the centre of government. Like all large towns, it had theatres, restaurants and bath-houses, where people could relax and be entertained.

VILLAGES AND TRADE

SOUTH ASIA

Most people in India lived in villages. In the dry north-west, farmers grew crops such as wheat and chickpeas, and lived in houses made of sun-baked mud brick. In the hot, rainy south they grew rice, pepper, spices, mangoes and coconuts. Their houses had bamboo walls with roofs made of palm leaf thatch.

Indian craftworkers made jewellery, glassware, metalwork and leather goods. Indian cloth had been famous in Europe and the Middle East since Roman times. In 1498 Vasco da Gama was the first European to sail around the south of Africa to reach India's west coast trading ports. Others soon followed and trade with Europe increased.

HUNTERS AND GATHERERS

AUSTRALASIA

Over thousands of years, the Aboriginal people of Australia had learned to survive in a harsh environment. People sometimes ate kangaroos, emu, shellfish, turtles, roasted moths, possums and birds' eggs. But mostly they ate plants, such as grass seeds, berries and yams. Women also dug up lizards and insect grubs for food. Most people were nomads. They moved from camp to camp, reaching each one when the local food supply of birds, fish, insects and plants was at its best.

MAORI FORTS AND FARMS

Many of the Maori people of New Zealand were farmers. They lived in villages, called pa, which were defended against enemies by wooden fences or stone walls. On the warm North Island the Maoris grew kumara, an orange-fleshed sweet potato. On the South Island, where it is colder and wetter, people fished, and trapped seabirds. Everywhere, Maori people gathered bracken roots, dried them, ground them up and cooked them with water to make a sticky paste.

▼ Aboriginal hunters used spears and boomerangs (throwing sticks) to catch many different wild animals for food. They were expert at following tracks and setting traps. This painting was made by a European artist in 1817 and shows ancient Aboriginal hunting techniques. The hunters are hiding behind trees and bushes ready to attack some kangaroos.

LIVING WITH THE ENVIRONMENT

AMERICAS

The landscape and climate of North America ranges from snowy mountains to tropical swamps, and from rocky desert canyons to wide, windswept prairies. So the Native American peoples who lived there had very different lifestyles. Some, like the Chinook on the north-west coast, lived in wooden houses and caught fish. Others, like the Hopi in the far south-west, lived in apartment blocks made of sun-dried bricks called adobe. They grew crops on irrigated lands. The Secotan lived in woodlands along the east coast. They hunted deer, caught fish and grew fields of maize.

THE CENTRE OF THE EMPIRE

The Aztec capital city of Tenochtitlán was surrounded by man-made floating gardens called chinampas, made of woven branches and mud from the lake bottom. Here farmers grew crops such as avocados, tomatoes, peppers and chillies. The Aztecs' staple food was maize, which they made into crispy pancakes and ate with spicy vegetable stew. People could also buy delicacies at the city market, such as cocoa powder, which they used to make a drink called 'chocolatl'.

▲ This picture was painted by an English traveller in about 1580. It shows a village built by the Secotan people. The houses are built of wood, with roofs made of waterproof tree-bark and woven straw.

◄ A silver statue of a llama made by an Inca craftworker in Peru.

INCA LIFESTYLE

Most Inca people lived in steep mountain valleys, or on high windswept plains, where only a few crops, such as potatoes, could grow. Farmers kept herds of llama and alpaca. Women wove llama hair into warm cloaks and blankets. The Incas had no wheeled transport, so they also used llamas to carry heavy loads up steep mountain tracks.

DISCOVERY AND INVENTION

Leonardo lived at a time when European scientists were challenging many of the teachings they had learned from the Church and at universities. They wanted to observe the world, make experiments and find out things for themselves. They made many important discoveries, especially in astronomy and anatomy.

One of the most important inventions during this time was the printing press. The invention of printing meant that more people could read about new ideas more quickly than before. Soon news of inventions and discoveries, including information about life outside Europe, was beginning to spread through many lands. More people were beginning to explore the world in the hope of making money from trade and treasure.

◄ Printing workshops were set up in many European cities. Printers arranged individual letters, made of metal or wood, to make up words on a page. At first they printed copies of the Bible and other religious writings. But by the 1500s they were also printing books on travel and science, maps, diaries and plays.

THE PRINTING PRESS

The first large-scale printing workshop in Europe was set up by Johann Gutenberg, in the German city of Mainz, in about 1450. It held six new printing presses with movable type. Printing was not a European invention. The Chinese had discovered how to do it hundreds of years before. But because their language has more than 2,000 characters, Chinese scholars found it quicker to copy out books by hand.

THE GREAT EXPLORERS

Christopher Columbus was not the the first person to think the world was round. But he was the first to try and reach India and the Far East by sailing west from Europe, across the uncharted Atlantic Ocean. The king and queen of Spain gave him money for the journey, because they wanted to find a new trade route for their Spanish ships. Columbus crossed the Atlantic in 1492. He did not realize that he had, in fact, landed in the Americas, and not in India.

NEW SCIENCE

In 1543 a Polish astronomer called Nicolaus Copernicus published a book saying that the earth moved round the sun. Before this, people thought that the earth was at the centre of the universe. Also in 1543 a Belgian doctor called Vesalius published the first European book with pictures of the human body and diagrams of how bones and muscles work.

AROUND THE WORLD

The first voyage round the world was planned by a Portuguese soldier called Ferdinand Magellan. He set off from Spain in 1519 with five ships and 237 crew. Although he was killed in the Philippines, the voyage was completed by Captain Sebastian del Cano. He arrived home in 1522, after three years at sea, with only one ship and 17 members of the original crew alive.

◄ In the 1400s and 1500s, bigger, stronger ships were built to carry explorers on long voyages. This ship has big square sails to catch the wind. It is armed with cannon to fight off pirates.

▼ A diagram showing Copernicus' new ideas. The sun (with a face) is in the centre, with the planets around it. Earth is shown as a blue and green globe above the sun.

AN IMPORTANT DRINK

MIDDLE EAST

Coffee trees first grew naturally in north-east Africa. But in the 1400s, Arab traders brought coffee seedlings from Ethiopia to grow coffee plantations in Arabia. The habit of drinking coffee became very fashionable. It spread throughout the Muslim world, carried home by travellers who had made a pilgrimage to the holy city of Mecca. Over the centuries that followed, coffee-drinking has spread worldwide. Coffee is now the second most important item, after oil, in international trade.

▲ Cannon changed warfare and made traditional city defences almost useless. This picture shows an Ottoman army with its cannon, cannonballs and gunpowder barrels.

BIG GUNS

Guns and cannon were used more and more in Europe and the Middle East in Leonardo's time, and the Ottomans made some of the best cannon in the world. The largest were made of bronze and could fire a heavy cannon ball at targets more than a kilometre away. They could be up to 6.5 metres long, and cast in two pieces. Sultan Mehmet II used cannon like these to smash the walls of Constantinople, which had survived all other attacks for more than a thousand years.

◄ This Turkish miniature shows guests drinking coffee at a banquet. Servants are busy with coffee cups on the right, towards the back. Behind them, the host entertains his most important guests.

BUILDING IN A HOT WET CLIMATE

AFRICA

In West Africa builders had to cope with a hot climate and heavy rains. The local building materials were sun-baked mud, used to make the walls, and palm-leaf thatch, for the roof. To stop the walls from being washed away in the rain, the leaf roof hung over the edges. People built rooms round an open courtyard so that only a small roof was needed on each side. If they had built square houses with a wide single roof, the leaves would have soaked up too much water, and collapsed.

DRY-STONE WALLS

In the rocky uplands of East Africa, people used a technique called dry-stone walling. Small blocks of a hard stone called granite were cut into shape with sharp iron tools, then arranged in decorative patterns. Only skilful shaping and laying held the blocks in place. The builders did not use cement.

DANGEROUS EXPERIMENTS

EAST ASIA

Before Leonardo's time, Chinese emperors had encouraged great inventors and explorers. Chinese porcelain, explosives, paper and silk were famous in many lands. Chinese sailors may even have explored as far as Australia. After about 1430, the expeditions stopped, and scientists made no great discoveries for the next 100 years. But a few inventors still tried out new ideas. In 1500 a scientist called Wu Han tried to use gunpowder to launch a rocket that would let him fly through the air. It exploded and he was killed.

SAMURAI ARMOUR

In Japan, many years of war led to changes in samurai armour. Important warriors still wore splendid armour at court, but on the battlefield they needed something more practical. Usually they fought on foot with swords, so they needed armour that allowed them to move easily. During the late 1400s, a lightweight armour was developed, made of little metal plates sewn on to cloth. Once guns began to be used in Japan, in 1543, inventors designed bullet-proof armour made of hinged iron plates.

▶ Samurai armour was often destroyed in battle, so little survives. But high-ranking warriors kept armour like this, to wear at important ceremonies. It was made out of leather and flexible iron plates. The face was shielded by a fierce iron mask. It was much heavier than battle armour.

GUNS AND SIEGE WARFARE

When the Mughal leader Babur invaded India and founded an empire, his soldiers carried cannon with them, and hand-held guns. They also rode on horseback, in the traditional Mongol way. These horses and guns gave Babur's soldiers a great advantage over the local Indian troops. The Indian armies fought on foot, and their weapons were bows and arrows, spears and swords. Although they also had war-elephants, which usually terrified enemy foot soldiers, Babur's soldiers on their light, nimble horses simply galloped out of the elephants' way.

KNOWING THE SEA

The Pacific peoples were skilled boatbuilders and expert navigators. They used the sun and moon, clouds, currents and the flight of sea-birds to help them steer. They made maps of the ocean, using sticks to mark fast currents, and shells and stones to mark islands.

FISHING SKILLS

Aboriginal fishermen developed simple but effective techniques to help them work. They used fishing spears tipped with lots of small points (like a very sharp comb) so that a fish could not slip off. They also lit small fires on board their canoes. At dusk the smoke kept biting insects away, and at night the light attracted the fish towards them.

NEW FOODS

European explorers sailed to America in search of treasure, and found vegetables and spices unknown to the rest of the word. Farmers in America had discovered how to grow crops of maize, potatoes, tomatoes, cocoa, chillies, kidney beans and sweet peppers. These plants all first arrived in Europe in the 1500s, along with sunflowers, pineapples and turkeys. Maize was also introduced into Africa and China. Hot, spicy chillies soon became an important ingredient in food in India and the nearby lands.

◄ When Babur attacked Indian towns he used new technology, which you can see in this picture. His soldiers built zigzag walls to hide the cannons, and wood and leather screens for soldiers to hide behind. They dug covered trenches, called sabat, so that soldiers could creep close to enemy walls without being shot at by their enemies high above. Bullocks are pulling more cannon up the hill.

MEDICINES

Doctors in the Americas developed their own medical treatments. They made up soothing mixtures of local herbs and used tobacco as a medicine. The Aztecs of Central America used chillies as a painkiller and an antiseptic. They also gave people sweat-baths, where patients sat in a hot, steamy hut, like a sauna.

Inca doctors learned how to 'trepan' or cut holes in a patient's skull, to relieve pressure on the brain from head injuries. The Incas may also have been the first people in the world to carry out blood transfusions. Because many Native peoples in South America shared the same blood group, there were few problems finding matching donors.

▲ The Aztecs kept notes of medical treatments. This picture from an Aztec book called a codex shows a nurse massaging a patient, and a doctor giving someone some medicine.

▼ The ruins of Machu Picchu, an Inca city high in the Andes Mountains. The straw roofs have gone, but the stone walls have survived 500 years and many earthquakes.

INCA BUILDINGS

The Inca city of Cuzco was built in the Andes Mountains. Because Cuzco is so high above sea level, few trees grow there and everything, from huge temples and palaces to peasant huts, had to be built of stone. There were also many earthquakes, so Inca stonemasons developed earthquake-proof buildings. They cut the stone into massive blocks and smoothed the edges using stone tools. Then they fitted the blocks tightly together like a giant jigsaw puzzle to build the walls. They did not use mortar. When there was an earthquake, all the stones jumped and shifted a little, then settled back into place. The roofs were made of dried mountain grass.

THE CREATIVE WORLD

During Leonardo's lifetime, people all over the world began to be more aware of works of art from distant lands. More people were travelling further than before, and explorers and traders took home exotic goods of all kinds. When the Spanish explorer Cortez returned from Mexico, he presented Emperor Charles V with a magnificent Aztec headdress, made of precious bird feathers. European artists often painted luxury objects, such as carpets from the Middle East, in their pictures to create rich and impressive backgrounds.

Indian and Turkish artists began to copy beautiful miniature paintings from Persia. Skilled craftworkers in Benin soon began to include figures of Portuguese explorers among the bronze portrait sculptures they made.

▶ This famous statue, called the *Pietà*, was carved by an Italian artist called Michelangelo Buonarotti. It shows the Virgin Mary cradling the dead Jesus Christ. Michelangelo was a skilful sculptor and painter. He mixed Renaissance ideas of human beauty with traditional Christian beliefs.

THE RENAISSANCE

EUROPE

In the 1400s and 1500s European painters and sculptors began to work in a new style. It was more lifelike and more dramatic than art had ever been before. It also showed human feelings in a new, direct way. People called this new style a 'Renaissance' of art. (Renaissance is a French word meaning rebirth.) These new ideas and styles spread quickly from Italy where they began, to the rest of Europe.

RENAISSANCE IDEAS

Renaissance artists and scholars studied ancient Greek and Roman books. From their studies they developed a new way of thinking called humanism. The humanists believed that respect for human beings, their ideas and achievements, was more important than faith in a remote mysterious god. They tried to show these beliefs in their work.

▲ Hans Holbein was a German painter who spent many years working in England. He painted this picture, called *The Ambassadors*, for King Henry VIII. The men are shown in a lifelike way. The globes, books and musical instruments show that they were interested in Renaissance arts, science and ideas.

► Alessandro Botticelli was another Renaissance artist, who lived and worked in Florence. He often copied ancient Greek and Roman designs. This is a detail from one of his paintings. It shows Primavera, the Roman goddess of spring.

ART AND NATURE

Two things helped Renaissance artists create a new style. First they studied ancient Greek and Roman paintings and sculptures, and learned how to copy their lifelike designs. They also copied their buildings, and built churches and palaces to look like Greek and Roman temples. Second, like Leonardo, they studied nature carefully. They tried to show human bodies, plants and animals in as real a way as possible.

Some artists explored the way our eyes look at things and invented a new painting technique called perspective. This allowed painters to show space and distance inside a picture, even though the painting itself was flat.

OTTOMAN ART

Sultan Suleiman (see page 20), wore glittering jewels and beautiful clothes. His palace in Istanbul was filled with the best glassware and metalwork that the artists and craftworkers of his empire could supply. The palace walls had panels of tiles glazed in bright colours and complicated patterns. The walls were also hung with the finest carpets. The palace gardens were carefully designed and full of sweet-smelling roses and carnations.

▼ This Persian miniature shows a scholar and his pupils. The Ottomans and Indians admired Persian designs, and students often travelled to Persia to study with top artists.

▲ The gardens of Sultan Suleiman's palace. In this Turkish miniature, painted in 1524, you can see courtiers strolling around the grounds, sheltering in a tower and admiring the rare trees and flowers.

BOOKS AND MINIATURES

The Ottomans gave large sums of money to pay for mosques and tombs. They also encouraged artists to make beautiful books, written in decorative handwriting called calligraphy. The books were bound with leather and studded with precious jewels. Like their neighbours the Persians, the Ottomans admired and collected miniatures. These were detailed little paintings in bright colours. They often showed scenes from traditional stories, or of life at the royal court.

AFRICAN BRONZES AND CARVINGS

AFRICA

By Leonardo's time, Benin craftworkers had perfected a technique of making beautiful, realistic statues from bronze or brass. They also made bronze plaques, which showed scenes from traditional stories and historic events, and recorded important ceremonies. They were used to decorate the walls and gateways of palaces belonging to the oba and to powerful chiefs.

African craftworkers also created many brightly-coloured textiles, woven from wool and cotton. They made masks and sculptures carved from local materials.

► West African craftworkers made many beautiful objects from precious ivory and tropical woods. This ivory mask was used by the obas of Benin during religious ceremonies. It was worn hanging from a belt.

MING CHINA

EAST ASIA

Chinese merchants had sold fine china, called porcelain, to Europe for many years. In Leonardo's time craftworkers at the emperor's factory developed a new way of working that allowed them to add bright touches of colour to the glaze after it had been fired. Some of the finest Ming porcelain was made for the emperor's court. But most was specially designed to sell in Africa, the Middle East and Europe, to earn money for China abroad.

POEMS AND MANUSCRIPTS

SOUTH ASIA

In India, the new Mughal emperors were keen to encourage the arts. Babur, the Mughal conqueror, was a poet. He was also a collector of fine books and manuscripts. Sometimes pictures of birds and flowers were pasted into albums to decorate the text. The palace library held thousands of volumes, and was one of the largest in the world.

Babur also liked beautiful surroundings. He employed teams of workmen and architects to design flowery meadows and cool, shady gardens with ponds and fountains, where he could relax in the heat of the Indian summer, admire delicate flowers, and eat delicious fruits.

► By the 1400s one of the most famous styles of Ming porcelain was a blue-and-white china, patterned with plants, flowers, animals or scenes with people. This vase shows Chinese people at a feast in a garden.

▲ The ruins of Vittala Temple, from the Vijayanagar Empire. It was designed to look like the sun god's chariot.

THE CITY OF VIJAYANAGAR

SOUTH ASIA

In southern India, the Hindu kings who ruled the Vijayanagar Empire paid for beautiful palaces and temples to be built. Visitors said the city of Vijayanagar was spectacular. It covered more than 23 square kilometres, and had lakes, canals, fruit-gardens and seven encircling city walls. The king's palace was decorated with carvings of roses and lotus-flowers.

MUSIC AND FESTIVALS

AUSTRALASIA

Music was an important part of life for many people around the world. The Aboriginal people of Australia held special festivals of music and dancing. They sang songs and told stories that had been passed on by word of mouth for thousands of years. They danced to the music of the didgeridoo, a hollow wooden tube which was blown to produce a deep humming sound.

Maori craftworkers in New Zealand carved flutes and whistles from wood or bone. They made wooden gongs, and trumpets out of conch shells. They also carved detailed patterns in wood to decorate houses, gateways and canoes.

◄ Carved wooden panels like this one were used to decorate Maori chiefs' houses. This is from the top section of a wooden door frame.

BODY PAINTING

In North America there were many different kinds of art. People made totem poles, leatherwork and pottery objects. Many people painted their bodies with detailed patterns. They made paints from plants and crushed earth. The patterns were a sign of adulthood, and also showed that the wearer belonged to a particular group in society. Often art had a religious purpose. The Hopi and Navajo people created beautiful pictures out of sand, showing the spirits of earth and sky. These were made as part of a ritual to heal sick people. When the ritual was over, the painting was destroyed.

the manner of their attire and painting them selues when they goe to their generall huntings, or at theire Solemne feasts.

► A mask made of a thin sheet of gold, hammered into a face shape. Masks like this were made in several parts of the Inca empire, especially by the Chimu people. They were often used to cover the faces of dead people.

▲ This Native American chief was painted in 1585 by John White, one of the first European artists to travel to America. The chief has decorated his body with purple patterns.

INCA CRAFTWORKERS

In South America, the Inca emperors employed craftworkers to weave cloth, mould pottery and make delicate jewellery out of gold and precious stones. Men and women wore jewelled headbands, earrings, nose-studs and chest-ornaments. In Cuzco, the Inca capital city, the biggest temple had a sacred garden full of lifesize animals and food-plants made of real gold.

Inca metalworkers had an honoured place in the community. Their sons were trained to work with them from a very early age, because it took many years to learn their skills.

INCA MUMMIES

The Incas and other South American peoples believed that silver was the tears of the moon, and that gold was the sweat of the sun. They also believed that gold had magical qualities. People used it to make masks to cover the faces of dead emperors, before they were made into mummies and buried. Inca mummies were dressed in rich robes and wrapped in fine-woven cloth. On festival days, people took the mummies from their tombs and carried them through the streets.

BELIEFS AND IDEAS

I n Leonardo's time, almost everyone in the world believed in some kind of religion. In many lands, laws, scholarship and education were all based on religious ideas. The biggest, most beautiful buildings were designed for religious use, and all the year round, there were rituals and festivals that made men, women and children feel closer to the gods. Religion was also closely linked to politics. In many countries, people of the same faith quarrelled and even fought each other over their different religious opinions.

► Martin Luther preaching to people who shared his wish for a reformed Church. Preaching was an important way to spread new ideas. This is a detail of a picture painted on strips of wood.

THE REFORMATION

There were many quarrels about religion in Leonardo's time. Almost everyone in Europe followed the Christian faith, and in western Europe people belonged to the Roman Catholic Church. It was rich and powerful, and its leader, the pope, played an important part in politics. But religious reformers complained that the Church was corrupt and that priests were lazy. They demanded the freedom to worship God in a new way. Reformers wanted to hold church services and read the Bible in their own languages, instead of in Latin, so that people could understand more about their faith.

In the 1400s and 1500s the reformers set up new churches of their own, led by campaigners such as Martin Luther in Germany and John Calvin in Switzerland. They became known as Protestants, because of their complaints and protests about the Roman Catholic faith.

SPIRIT MASKS

By Leonardo's time, many nations in North Africa had been converted to Islam. Elsewhere, people kept their own ancient beliefs. They believed in one god, who had made the world, and in other lesser gods and spirits.

Most people believed that dead ancestors had the power to help or harm them. Ancestors' bones, or carved masks representing ancestor spirits, were sometimes kept in a special house in the village. On festival days the masks were carried through streets and fields by men who were members of secret societies, based on family groups or certain trades. Women belonged to secret societies, too. Often, they trained their members in healing skills.

FAITH OF ISLAM

People in the Middle East followed the faith of Islam. But the two most powerful ruling families, the Ottomans and the Safavids (in Persia) belonged to different branches of the faith. They disagreed over who should lead the Muslim community. Religious disagreement mixed with political rivalry and caused many years of fighting between them.

▲ When the Ottomans conquered Constantinople in 1453, they turned its famous Christian church, called Santa Sophia, into a mosque.

RELIGIOUS TOLERANCE

The Ottomans were tolerant towards people of other faiths living in their empire so long as they obeyed Ottoman laws. Ottoman governors worked with Christian leaders to set up a system of local government, which collected taxes and kept law and order in conquered lands.

SHINTOISM

EAST ASIA

In Japan, most people followed the ancient Shinto faith. They worshipped many spirits, including gods and goddesses, the souls of past warriors, emperors and famous scholars, their family ancestors and the spirits who lived in mountains, rocks and trees. People visited Shinto shrines to ask these divine beings to protect them. Priests who lived at the shrines had powers to bless worshippers. Sometimes they also told people their fortunes.

ZEN BUDDHISM

A new branch of Buddhism had been introduced to Japan from China around 1200. It was called Zen. By Leonardo's time, it had become very popular. Zen beliefs and Shinto traditions mixed to form a new set of beliefs, which stressed honour, duty and respect for national leaders.

▼ Japanese Zen Buddhists made stone gardens like this one, where people could meditate. They believed this would help people think clearly and behave well.

A NEW FAITH

SOUTH ASIA

People in India followed different faiths. Most were Hindus, but there were also Muslims, Buddhists, Parsees and Jains. In Leonardo's time a new religion grew up in India: the Sikh faith. It was founded by Guru Nanak, who was born in north-west India in 1469. As a young man he travelled around the country, urging people to think about God by singing religious songs.

Nanak became known as Guru, which means 'Holy Teacher'. His words were respected by Hindus and Muslims, but soon after Guru Nanak's death, his followers broke away from other religious groups, and began to worship in their own Sikh way.

ISLAM IN ASIA

Elsewhere in South Asia, on the islands of present-day Malaysia and Indonesia, many people were being converted to the faith of Islam. They learned about it from Muslim spice traders who came to their countries from the Middle East.

NATURE GODS

In the islands of Hawaii, people worshipped the spirits who controlled waves, storms and volcanoes. They made statues of them out of woven branches and built stone altars, where they offered sacrifices.

In Australia, Aboriginal people believed that long ago, in the Dreamtime, ancestors of all creatures wandered across the earth, linking everything together in a peaceful whole. Aboriginal people held ceremonies at holy sites to recreate the ancestors' wanderings and to bring peace and order to the world.

► This Native American healer, called a shaman, was painted by John White in about 1580. Shamans healed sick people and brought good fortune by being in touch with magic spirits. To do this, they chanted and danced until they fell into a trance.

FEEDING THE SUN

The Aztecs of Mexico believed they had to offer prayers to the gods, and feed them with human blood, or the world would come to an end. When they built a new temple in honour of the sun god, in the Aztec city of Tenochtitlán, more than 20,000 captives were sacrificed over several days.

▼ The Aztecs believed in many gods. This is the sun god, shown wearing a headdress of feathers.

EARTH AND MOON

The Incas of South America also worshipped the sun, and many other nature gods, including Mother Earth and Mother Moon. They honoured the gods with singing and dancing, and offered sacrifices to them. They believed that if they did not do this, the gods would punish them by sending earthquakes, or by making their crops die in the fields.

GUARDIAN SPIRITS

The Incas believed that everyone had a guardian spirit, which they called a huauqui. This belief was shared by many North American peoples, too. They went off into a quiet place, prayed, fasted and sometimes took drugs, and hoped the spirit would contact them.

GLOSSARY

PEOPLES FROM AROUND THE WORLD

Aboriginals The first inhabitants of Australia, who arrived there about 40,000 years ago.

Aztecs A civilization in Central America, powerful from about 1300 to 1521, when it was conquered by the Spanish.

Bedouin Nomads who live in Arabia and the dry, desert lands of the Middle East. They bred camels and kept flocks of sheep and goats.

Chimu A civilization in South America, conquered by the Incas in about 1300.

Chinook Native Americans who lived on the north-west coast of America. They lived by fishing for salmon and trading in shells.

Hopi Native Americans from the semi-desert regions of south-west North America. Some of their village sites have been occupied continuously for about 1000 years.

Incas A civilization in the Andes Mountains of South America that was powerful from 1200 to 1533, when it was conquered by the Spanish.

Inuit Native Americans who arrived in the Arctic regions of North America about 4000 years ago.

Maoris Settlers in New Zealand who came from the Pacific islands from about 800 AD.

Mongols Nomads who originally lived on the wide grassy plains north of China. Around 1200 they began to move south and west, conquering a vast empire. By Leonardo's time the Mongol Empire had been divided into four smaller, weaker kingdoms.

Native Americans The first inhabitants of America, who arrived there about 30,000 years ago. Native American people were divided into many nations with different lifestyles and languages.

Navajo Native American hunters and gatherers who migrated to live as farmers in the dry semi-desert lands of south-west North America around 1400.

San Hunters and gatherers who have lived in the deserts of southern Africa for thousands of years. By Leonardo's time some of their lands were occupied by Khoikhoi and Bantu-speaking people from the north.

Secotan Native Americans who lived on the south-east coast of North America in present-day South Carolina. They grew crops of maize and hunted deer in the woods.

administrator Someone who organizes things.
anatomy The study of the body and how it works.
ancestor A long-dead relative.
architecture Fine buildings.
the arts Music, art and literature.
astronomy The study of the sun, moon, planets and stars.

blood transfusion Giving one person blood taken from another.
Buddhism A religious faith founded by the Buddha, an Indian prince who lived in the sixth century BC. He taught his followers to seek truth and the right way to live by meditation.

Christianity A religious faith taught by Jesus Christ, a preacher who died around 30 AD. Christians believe Jesus is the son of God.
the Church The organization of the Christian religion. A church is a building where people worship.
citizen A person who lives in a city, and has rights as a member of the community.
city-state A city that also rules over the surrounding countryside, villages and farms.
civilization A society with its own laws, customs, beliefs and artistic traditions.
code A collection of laws.
coral A hard, often beautifully-coloured material formed by the skeletons of tiny sea animals.

diplomacy Skill in dealing with people and governments.
dynasty A ruling family.

earthwork A large mound, ditch, bank or circle made of earth dug from the surrounding land.

engineer Someone who studies how things work and invents new machines.

frescoes Pictures painted directly on a freshly-plastered wall.

glazed Covered with a smooth, glassy coating. Glaze was used to make objects more beautiful.

governor The ruler of part of an empire or kingdom.

Hindu A person who follows the Hindu religion, which grew up in India between about 1500–600 BC. Hindus worship many gods.

Holy Roman Emperor An ancient title given to kings who ruled over a large part of Europe.

irrigate To channel water into dry land, so crops can grow there.

Islam The worship of Allah (God), taught by Muhammad, a prophet who lived in Arabia from 570–632 AD. Followers of Islam are called Muslims.

Jains People who follow the teachings of Mahavira, a holy man who lived in the sixth century BC. Jains try not to harm any person, bird, animal, insect or plant.

jester An entertainer who made people laugh.

looted Stolen by an invading army.

manuscript A book written and beautifully decorated by hand.

merchant A person who buys and sells goods.

Middle East The area that stretches eastwards from the Mediterranean Sea towards Asia.

meditation Thinking deeply about spiritual things.

missionary A person who travels to another country to teach about their religious beliefs.

mosque A building where Muslims meet to pray and study.

Muslim A follower of the religion of Islam.

nomads People who have no settled home, and who move from place to place in search of food, water and grazing land.

oba A king from the African kingdom of Benin.

Parsees People who follow the teachings of Zoroaster, who lived in Persia around 600 BC. Parsees worship Ahura Mazda and see the world as a battleground between good and evil forces.

patron Someone who spends money to pay for new works of art, music or literature.

pearl oyster A shellfish that produces pearls by coating anything that gets into its shell with a beautiful, shiny coating, called nacre.

peasant A person, usually poor, who lives and works in the countryside.

philosophy The study of ideas, knowledge and wisdom.

plaque A kind of plate with writing or carving on it, usually fixed to a wall.

ransom Money demanded by soldiers or criminals as payment for setting prisoners free.

Reformation A religious movement, strong in northern Europe in the 1500s and 1600s. Religious reformers wanted freedom to worship in their own way and an end to corruption in the Roman Catholic Church.

Renaissance A period in the 1400s and 1500s when people explored new ideas and artistic styles. A typical Renaissance person was interested in all areas of knowledge, including art, science, music and travel.

republic A place ruled by elected leaders, not by a king or queen.

ritual Traditional way of marking a special, often religious event.

Roman Catholic A branch of the Christian religion, based in Rome, in Italy, with the pope as its leader.

sauna A hot steam bath.

scholar Someone who spends their time studying.

sultan The Arabic word for king.

taxes Payments made to a government or ruler to pay for running the country.

technology The science of developing tools and techniques to meet practical needs.

terracotta Clay that has been baked in a special oven called a kiln at a fairly low temperature. It is usually a brick-red colour.

tolerant (of religion) to allow people to follow their own faith and worship in their own way.

trade route A long-distance route used by travelling merchants.

trading post A place where merchants meet to trade.

tribute Valuable goods paid to rulers by conquered people.

INDEX

Aboriginals 16, 22, 28, 34, 40, 45, 46
Africa 14, 20, 26, 33, 39, 43
Americas 17, 23, 29, 34-5, 41, 45
ancestor spirits 43, 45
apprenticeships 5
armour, Samurai 33
Atahualpa of the Incas 17
Australasia 16, 22, 28, 34, 40, 45
Aztecs 17, 23, 29, 35, 45, 46

Babur of the Mughals 16, 22, 34, 39
Bedouin people 26, 46
Benin, Africa 14, 20, 26, 39
body painting 41
building techniques 33, 35

cannon warfare 32, 34
Cano, Sebastian del 31
Chimu people 41, 46
China 15, 21, 27, 33, 39
Chinook people 29, 46
coffee-drinking 32
Columbus, Christopher 31
Constantinople 13, 32, 43
Copernicus, Nicolaus 31
creative work 36-41
Cuzco (Inca city) 35, 41

discoveries 30-5
dry-stone walling 33

East Asia 15, 21, 27, 33, 39, 44
Esigie of Benin 20
Europe 13, 19, 25, 31, 37, 43
explorers 14, 31

farming 25, 26, 27, 28, 29, 34
fishing techniques 34
Florence, Italy 5, 7, 19, 24

guardian spirits 45
gun warfare 32, 34
Gutenberg, Johann 31

Hawaii 45
Henry VIII of England 19
Hopi people 29, 41, 46
humanism 37
Hundred Years War 12, 13
hunting and gathering lifestyles 28

Idia of Benin 20
Incas 17, 23, 29, 35, 41, 46
India 16, 22, 28, 34, 39-40, 44
inventions 30-5
Islam religion 43, 44, 47

Japan 15, 21, 27, 33, 44

leaders 18-23
Leonardo da Vinci 4-7
lifestyles 24-9
Luther, Martin 43

Magellan, Ferdinand 31
Maoris 22, 28, 40, 46
medical treatments 35
Medici, Lorenzo de 19
Mehmet II of the Ottomans 20, 32
Middle East 13-14, 20, 25-6, 32, 38, 43
Ming dynasty 15, 21, 39
miniatures 38
Mona Lisa 7
Mongols 21, 46
Montezuma II of the Aztecs 23
Mughal dynasty 22, 34, 39
mummies, Inca 41
musical skills 40

Nanak, Guru 44
Native Americans 17, 29, 41, 46
nature gods 45
navigation skills 34
New Zealand 22, 28, 40
nomad lifestyle 26

obas of Benin 14, 20
Oda Nobunaga of Japan 21
Ottomans 13-14, 20, 32, 38, 43
Ozuolua of Benin 20

Pachacuti of the Incas 23
porcelain 39
poverty 25
printing 30, 31

Reformation 43, 47
religious beliefs 42-5
Renaissance 37, 47
rice growing 27

samurai warriors 15, 33
San people 26, 46
Secotan people 29, 46
shamans 45
Shintoism 44
shogun leaders 21
Sikh faith 44
South Asia 16, 22, 28, 34, 39-40, 44
spirit masks 43
Suleiman I of the Ottomans 20, 38
sun worship 45

Tenochtitlán (Aztec city) 17, 29
town life 25, 26, 27, 29
trading 14, 16, 25, 26, 28

Verrocchio, Andrea 5, 19
Vesalius, Andreas 31
Vijayanagar, India 40
village life 25, 26, 28

Wars of the Roses 13

Zen Buddhism 44